Sovereignty of the mind

By Laodicah Nyaribari

Chapter one:

Yes we can!

To get to the Promised Land, you have to negotiate your way through the wilderness. Your real world is a giant negotiating table, and like it or not you are participants-it's only you to package and brand your main concern in life. This depends on the sovereignty of your individual mind.

It's you to use what you have got to get what you want. The brain is the biggest asset that you ever have got .It only depends on how you engage it..... Negative or positive pole. People get locked into a rut of trying harder without trying smart. Trying hard doesn't always work. Sometimes, we need to do some things radically different to achieve greater levels of success. We need to break out of paradigm prisons, our habit patterns and from our comfort zones. Know and understand that everybody can be great..... because anybody can serve. You don't have to have a college degree to become, belong and serve. You don't have to make your subject and verb agree to serve. You only need a heart full of grace. A soul generated by love. All you should understand and get clear is this: That it is better to be prepared for an opportunity and not have one, than to have an opportunity and not be prepared. The biggest question therefore is whether you are going to be able to say a hearty Yes to your adventure.

And in either way you are always right! You have got to understand who you are, what you want and where you are really going. And what you have is within you. Whatever we are looking for was never on land or at sea. It's within your potential and your reach to get to where you want to go. It's a grievous mistake that quite often we do not understand what we exactly want in life. This is because we are trying all things through trial and error method.

However there are questions that we should always ask ourselves:

- **What do I really want?**
- **How does it affect my life (is it a plus or a negative pole)?**
- **Does it reflect the weights lifted inside out?**
- **Are you ready to die by your own sword fighting for your goals, ideas, dreams and aspirations?**

Without a deep, core passion to anchor your efforts, it will be tough to stay the course when adversity and disappointments rain down. Are we the type with a habit of malicious obedience? Not ready and willing to do things differently? Bear in mind that the sense of obligation to continue, to exist is present in all of us. It's not a question of vegetating. A duty to strive is the duty of us all. We are entitled to that calling as a duty.

The secret of walking on water is knowing where the stones are. Unreality is the true source of powerlessness. What we do not understand, we cannot control said Richard Reich. Unless we have engaged our minds properly, all we will be doing will be but chasing winds for years on end without realizing our goals. This of course brings us to an ever ending platform of finger pointing, blame games and fault finding in other people. Remember that you are you, you are who you are and you will never be equal to anybody else. Everybody has a purpose in life and we were all created so.

If life is a game, then definitely negotiating through the sovereignty of the mind is a way of life. If you want to succeed, you must try to comprehend the game in its entirety. Initially you must be reality oriented----- seeing things as they really are without passing judgement.The question that lingers is this: Are you a pessimist or an optimist?

Avoid this subjectivity, since it can only translate itself into wishful thinking. Rather see it like it is! The real you! Most of us are walking in other people's shadows. Remember you are with great potential, talents and full of gifts. There is nobody equal to you. You are original you. You can never be the same with so and so. Not even Siamese twins. It's you to take up the pen and write about your own story; nobody can ever do it for you. The pen is in your hands.

If you think you can or you can't you are always right said Henry Ford. And as long as you get there before it's over you are never late said James J.Walker. The meek shall inherit the earth.... But not its mineral rights said Paul Getty. Winning at all costs is our obligation and agenda. We should not be thinking of a win-lose situation in which the competitive struggle for admission to a good college can be just as rugged as the competition between MacDonald's and burger king. Some people interpret this to mean that all life is a constant battle of winning and losing. They see a world filled with rivals and competitors, with persons who want their job, their class, standing, their money, their promotion, their parking space or their spouse.

With our sovereign mind we can! We are tough battlers who seek to meet our own goals at all costs without worrying about the needs & the acceptance of others. There is no doubt in our minds that we are right in our conviction and approach.

For each of our victory brings a sense of exhilaration. It's not over until it's over. He is free who knows how to keep in his own hands the power to decide. Why should we question the monkey when you can question the organ grinder? Does the squeaky wheel really get the grease? Yes- if it knows where and how to squeaky. To resort to power of thinking and imagination, one need not to be violent (follow your heart), and to speak to conscience

one need to not be meek. The most effective action both resorts to power and engages conscience. Your life is the real you. Take it personally. Within our own life times, the accelerating pace of change and the increasing complexity of problems stagger even the expert. As a result, some people feel like strangers, like ciphers, lost in the crowd. Such an attitude is a curious blend of apathy and despair. The apt metaphor is Franz Kafkers, ***the Castle,*** with its red tape and faceless masses waiting in endless lines. It's as if we have become depersonalized, like minute particles of some great statistical census- working ants in the giant anthill of life. For you to make a journey to a destination which you have never visited before, you need a *Map.* The same can be said of our life. If you are to succeed in life from your civic, human, intellectual assets you need a life *Map.* But what if you are a traveler, arriving at your destination and discover that the town is much bigger than you ever imagined? What if there are many more streets than you were told about? More houses and more people than you expected? ***You would definitely feel lost and confused in the midst of the chaos.*** This is the predicament many of us find ourselves in. We have accumulated the civic, intellectual, human assets as useful resources we desire and in many cases we have even overshot our targets. To live a life that you will be proud of you have to know your mission and follow it. In living your purpose, you will feel satisfied that your time spent on earth was worthwhile. Start by determining what is most important for you as a person. Structure your life in order to fulfill it. Leave each day as if it were your only one. He who has a why to live for can bear almost anyhow said Nietzsche.
Mimicking and mugging, I was just a game myself, ignorant. I thought to be, was to name myself. Full of myself, how could I know myself? I emptied myself and became myself. Life situations dictate that we empty ourselves

from mere fiction self to authentic self. This can only happen if we understand the power of our mind.....Our sovereignty. Henry Ford once said.... *I have learned this at least by my experiment. That if one advances confidently in the direction of his dreams, and endeavors to live the life which he has imagined; he will meet with a success unexpected in common hours.*

We indeed create our own world by our ***thoughts.*** And thus we make our own heaven our own hell. It's true that we live in both mental (thoughts, ideas, concepts) and a physical world (actions, strategies, tactics).Most people are firmly planted in one realm or the others. Some focus too much on the physical side of things and as a result they succumb to the external pressures and events which cause them to live in a never ending cycle of struggles and strain. Aim for success, not perfection. Never give up your right to be wrong, because then you will lose the ability to learn new things and move forward with your life. If you wish success in life, make perseverance your bossom friend, experience your wise counselor, caution your elder brother and hope your guardian genius. Experience is not what happens to a man. It is what a man does with what happens to him. It's not actually what happens to you, it's what you do about. Our lives are a continuing journey and we must learn and grow at every bend as well make our way, sometimes stumbling, but always moving, toward the finest within us.

Remember that ideas are good but execution is everything. Very few people have what it takes to do it right. The only sure way to reach your goals is to be diligent and creative in the follow through. To reach new heights of achievement, you have to be present and mindful in the planning and implementation of the strategy.

Doing things the same old way is not going to get you anywhere except to the same old place. Having a firm commitment and passion for the idea will carry you through the times when you are weary of trying ***"one more time".*** For all you know, the next time may be you will finally succeed. Note that Ego and will power alone can't get you there. You have got to have ***Passion.*** Your future depends on many things, but ***mostly** on you.*

Nothing great in the world has ever been accomplished without ***passion.*** Remember as well, that luck happens when opportunity encounters ***the prepared sovereign mind.*** So ask the right questions and ask them now, not later. Sometimes we tend to ask ourselves enough questions but not the right questions. So ask the right questions. Obstacles are those frightful things you see when you take your eyes off your goal. Don't worry about the failure. Worry about the chances you miss when you don't even try. All you should know is this: Whether you think you can or think you can't you are always right. Now that we have come full circle, I trust the end of these journey marks the beginning of a rewarding and liberating phase of your life. You have a role to play in this world---- a reason for living here on earth. But it is up to you to find your part and direct your future.

You alone determine your destiny through your own efforts. Accept this ***responsibility.***

Not just for yourself, but for posterity. You have the power to change your life and the lives of others as well. Don't back away the exercise of power or want for someone else to act. Of course you can get what you want, but part of what you want should be to help others along the way.... Being our brothers' keeper and making the world a better place for everyone.

The good life is not a passive existence where you live and let live. It is one of involvement where you live and help live. Once you get into something, do it 100%.

As you wander on through life, sister/brother whatever be your goal, keep your eyes upon the donut and not upon the whole...... forget about glass ceilings, worry about glass walls.

The purpose of life is to be useful, to be responsible, to be honorable, and to be compassionate. It is, after all, to matter; to count, to stand for something, to have made some difference that you lived at all. Definitely you can through the power of the mind.

The best way to predict your future is to ***CREATE IT.*** 'Your actions should speak so loud that others shouldn't hear what you say'- words without commitment lose their coin. Words unsupported by action eventually prompt cynicism and despair.

Chapter two:

Fundamental principles of a sovereign mind:

Principle 1: Developing a positive mind:

There are two "people" walking around in each suit/set of clothes, each dress- ***the mind & the body.*** The part of the mind that you might call the captain of your ship is about the size of an eraser. Yet small as it is, when mind is exercised over matter powerful changes can occur. Unfortunately only 5% of the people let themselves be controlled by their minds. The other 95% are controlled by their bodies. In the same way, too, few of us are guided by faith, while too many of us are led by fear.

The mind says "Go ahead and be confident, you can do it, do it now." That is faith speaking, the first of the two most powerful words in the world.

The body says "hold back, you might fail, you can't do it, do it later". That is fear in your ear.

Today decides what you are going to be tomorrow. Today is what counts. Put out of your mind the fears, weaknesses and confidence-destroying thoughts of a week ago, a month ago and a year ago. Today is the day you must decide you will let the eraser sized portion of your mind- faith- control your body. Today is the day you banish your fear forever. But you ask how?

- Belief in yourself
- Associate with confident/successful people.
- Tune up your confidence machine.
- Be a master of your own ship.
- Keep busy. Not just being busy but being busy on what adds value to your life.
- Remember "you can get there from here" said Shirley Maclaine. The key word and principle is **you can!**

To succeed in life, maybe you need to change your attitudes too. As with everything else in life, there are recognizable opposites in attitude: - positive poles and negative poles, constructive and destructive, broad and narrow, cheerful and despairing. The secret you must learn and master is how to develop more positive attitudes toward yourself. This in turn will lead to more positive attitudes towards others. There are three basic rules to follow in order to develop more positive attitudes.

1. Widen your outlook:

We all look at life through some kind of mental glasses; beyond the ones we may actually wear to correct vision problems. Some people as we all know look through rose colored glasses and what they see is always or rather usually overly optimistic and entirely unrealistic.

Some people wear mental frames that pinch and they go through life with a constant headache to themselves and a headache to everyone else.

And some people wear mental contact lenses, invisible, but which like all contact lenses must be removed periodically. For them, part of life is always out of focus. Where are you as a person? Outlook! The way we look at life and through what glasses matters.

The song some people sing with their distorted vision is "dear me, the sky is falling" while others sing "everything is coming up roses". This depends so much on where you want to be a s a person. Nobody on earth can decide your destiny.

2. Turn yourself round:

This involves a degree of ***action.*** More than a degree, actually 180 degrees. A total ***reversal*** of any previous negative attitude. It's one thing to think positively and another to rid yourself of previous bad habits.

Unleashing of what might have been years of negative viewpoints, assumptions and perceptions takes time and effort. Any angle would do. It has to be 180 degrees angle on your campus of your life. This is majorly a mental action- link mental actions to physical ones- make a commitment.

3. Use your think power:

Use your think power in order to bring a lively and desired end. Put your thinking machine into gear. Think-power is a powerful staff and one of the secrets of developing a positive attitude of selling yourself more successfully. This lies in using that power to the highest degree." ***There is nothing either bad or good, but thinking makes it so" said William Shakespeare.*** You can fill your head with discouragement by thinking negative thoughts, or you can change your whole attitude about yourself and others by thinking positive thoughts. "Day by day in every way I'm getting better and better" - Emile Colle in his book Self mastery through consensus auto suggestion. His idea was: ***"think it and be it".***

Each day- each 1, 440 minutes is a new day. To think yourself into a new you. If the song you sing is "poor ***me, iam a nobody, friendless & un appreciated",*** that is the way others will sing it too.

On the other hand, if you think of yourself as a fairly nice person, someone/others would enjoy knowing you are pretty certain to come across that way. If in your mind's eye, you think of yourself as a friendly guy or person, chances are that's the way you will act."

The power to see ourselves as others see us". The truth is others see us as we ourselves- and think ourselves to be. The bible says "as a person thinketh so he is".

How you look at life is the way you look to others. One of the first steps in finding success in every endeavor is to widen your outlook toward people, places and events. The only kind of glasses you need to do is to get your own kind of binoculars. (Create and design yours).That will give you a broader perspective of life. By creating and designing your own binoculars, you will be dealing with what you understand within than just from without.

Analytical case:

The man who searched the heavens:

An Italian father gave his son a telescope on the occasion of his 10th birthday. The telescope was a replica of one used by sailors. The father used to call it a spy glass. This was fitting since the son spied a valuable lesson and took it to heart. One day the boy was using the spy glass when he complained and said "Father, this is useless. I can see better without it. Everything is too small". The father smiled. Of course, the boy was looking through the wrong end. It wasn't getting the big picture at all. He had the narrow outlook through the glass. The father gently TURNED the little telescope round. Now the father had widened the outlook and how fortunate that he did. The boy grew up and improved the little primitive telescope and with it discovered the moons of Jupiter, the rings of Saturn and the mountains on our moon. He became the world's foremost astronomer of his day. His name was Galileo.

To cut the story short, we need to discover as well. That to see things in proper perspective we must widen our outlook.

When you look at life, at others, at objects, at events, at your job, at your family, do you see the whole picture or only part of it? Do you examine both sides of a question?

Are you fair or are you judgemental? Are your perceptions bigoted or coloured? Do you keep an open mind?

Perhaps you are standing in the way of yourself.... Do prejudices either for or against something or someone throw the picture out of focus? Do you fail, as has been so often said, but wisely to see the forest for the trees?

Outlook means exactly what it says. Looking outward not inward, embracing others and ceasing to be self centered.

Start to see life as larger than yourself. Are you looking at both sides as you read this book right now? Do you mostly see the little picture and rarely the big picture? Have you made an effort to understand all the view points, all the shadings?

That widened outlook is a necessary step in developing positive attitudes that will help you succeed in life.

Principle 2:

Time-The equal opportunity employer:

Time is an equal opportunity employer. Don't try to save it. Time is the only resource or gift distributed equally to everyone. Each human being in every hemisphere and time zone has precisely 168 hours a week to spend.

It saddens as well as annoys at how we spend our time. Quite often it could be out of negligence, ignorance or outright obstinacy.

It's equally important to realize that time cuts down all both great and small - warned the new England premier three centuries ago. No one can ever buy another one hour. Scientists and computer experts can speed up data transmission to perform millions of transactions a second, but they can't create a single new second. None of us seems to have enough time, yet we all have there is or never will be. Life's raw materials spends itself now, this very moment- which is why how you really spend your time is far more important than all the material possessions you may own or positions you may attain. It's important to as well realize that there is no replay in the game of life. Time spent is gone forever. Each yesterday, and all of them together, are beyond your control. Literally all the money in the world can't undo or re-do a single act you performed. If we could really understand and get to the bottom line of the matter that we earnestly can't erase a single word you said, can't add an I love you, I' am sorry or I forgive you! Not even a thank you, you just forgot to say a while ago! You must spend your time wisely, but never try to save it. All this begins with a positive mind and a mind that is totally independent, by becoming the controller of your life and in shaping your own destiny. Remember, that it would take a hundred life times to accomplish all we are capable of, but we are just given one for learning and giving us much as we can, for doing our best.

If we had more time, there would be less need for books, less need to make plans and set priorities. If we had time forever, we could probably be living it every day and still end with immense knowledge, possibly even wisdom. But we are strictly limited to those 168 hours - 10,080 minutes a week, which is why Benjamin Franklin urged us not to squander "the staff life is made up of". Franklin coined the famous" time is money".

The celebrated German poet Johanna Goethe may have been a trifle opportunistic when he promised that "one always has enough time, if only one applies it well". The biggest question is; how well do we often utilize our time properly? Is itself directed or are we instructed on what to do at a particular time?

Time is an accepted truism. That time marches on. It moves at the same rate for all of us, no matter what we do. Since we cannot control the clock, we must examine how the passage of time affects the negotiation process. Always ask yourself: What will happen if I go beyond the deadlines? What is the certainty of the detriment or penalty? In short how great is the risk I'm taking? Note that time can be crucial to success. Time may even affect a relationship.

I. Accelerating with age:

One of life's great ironies is that time crawls when we are young, and flies as we age. When we were children, holidays took a long time to arrive! Then slowly at first, the clock began to accelerate. The 30th birthday seemed to arrive in explicably soon after the 25th . The fourthieth came altogether unexpectedly and less than a hearty welcome. At fourty you begin linking time to the seasons. At fifty you will realize that time appears to race with years because we understand how precious and rare it is and thus we begin appreciating our remaining portion as if it were pure oxygen escaping from a beautiful balloon that never refilled.

II. Only this moment:

Many people live in the past, wishing they could put the clock in reverse largely to undo mistakes. We can't relieve yesterday & mustn't waste today by living in a fantasy tomorrow.

Only the actions we take here and now can create tomorrow's real promise to become a sovereign individual we ought to be.

Principle3:

The best road traveled:

In our journey into the empires of our minds, we must remember that success is a process and not a destination, let alone a summit. To visualize the road best traveled you must understand that it's not what you have that counts- not your money, stocks, cars, position or estates. What counts is what you now do with what you have. Our society's current condition reminds me of another first line, this one by Charles Dickens -The famous "it was the best of times, it was the worst of times". This opens a tale of two cities, and could easily serve to summarize our own times.

You must always strive for excellence, but never seek perfection.

Which road is best according to you? As Robert Frost said, ***the road less traveled made all the difference!*** If that is the road you have chosen, never mind whether you are racing ahead, struggling on an upgrade or resting a moment while you catch your breath-You should know that life is not a book that is finished when you have read its last pages. You must do the important but delegate the urgent. Brother Jeremiah helps us to remember that life is to be lived and enjoyed. Therefore if you plan well then the right time to peak the daisies is definitely now! How do you go finding this roads less traveled? It's wise to remember that you can't find them in an atlas or on service station- station maps. It is harder than that, but also easier. They are roads ***you build yourself, roads that lead into your sovereign mind.***

And in one way or another you must travel the road you, yourself have designed. Then this will be the right time to start peaking the daisies! Why? It's something you very well understand. It suits your interest. It's your way of life. It's your dream and an inspiration of times. It's your priority. Go. go for it. Otherwise the law might be against it tomorrow.

While on the road less traveled, it's important to walk the talk. The comments that "your actions should speak louder that others can't hear what you say is the bottom line for all your operations to shape up your destiny. Remember that words without commitment lose their very coin. Words unsupported by action eventually prompt cynicism and despair.

Here are some action tips as you continue your journey on the road less traveled:

- Quality of the trip will always be more important than your final destination. Life is a journey, success is a process, not a pedestal on which to perch.
- Be willing to learn and to appreciate past challenges-Psychologist Rollo May advised that people should ***"rejoice in suffering, strange as it may sound, for this is the sign of the availability of energy to transform their characters".***
- Chose an attitude worthy of you in every situation. Don't take on what you do not fully understand. At your limit appreciate to progress and learn with an aim of succeeding.
- Start enjoying the ripple effect that comes with making a total difference.
- Enjoy the privilege of doing good. Doing good will give you the joy and satisfaction of even going beyond the expected limitations and this

brings together the synergies and effort so much required of a sovereign mind.

The continuing nature of the life process and our brief mortal encounter with it, calls for the cathedral perspective. It calls on us to gain hindsight from all that went before, which is history, with its failures, success, fashions, and traditions. It calls on us to gain foresight by imagining and imaging a better world a head for all by passing on our trials, errors and achievements as lessons in leadership. It calls on us to live in the present, longing for neither yesterday nor tomorrow, but rather facing what today offers, boldly, optimistically and flexibly.

Life like a cathedral, is not so much to be admired for its external appearance & majesty, although this are attractive and noteworthy. Life, like a cathedral, is more meaningful because of what goes on in ***the sanctity within.*** Hasten therefore to build your cathedrals or conquer your empires. Seek patiently to discover them by looking ***inward.***

You and I climb each Mount Everest in our lives every day as Edmund Hillary did his, because it's there no doubt! And also for the sheer exhilaration of testing our knowledge, skills and courage when we soul search deeply the meaning as to why we keep building the future, I recall what has been referred to as the cathedral perspective. The magnificent cathedrals we have, built in centuries past, most often took several life times to design and construct. Cathedrals take generations to build. So do great societies, companies, relations and even families.

Life is not something to step back from and admire when completed. It is an ongoing process of design, laying the foundations, forming, erecting, refining and renovating. We never get it quite right. That is why we need to face it with a lot of sovereignty of the mind. It is never perfect. it is always under ***construction.***

Principle 4:

Getting your cake and eating it through negotiation:

The independent mind brings power out of the ivory tower and down to the realities of getting things done. It helps you to learn how to be a person who doesn't shrink from the positive use of power to get what you want in life. Whatever you are negotiating for a raise, a home, a car or anything is a must for a better, more profitable and more satisfying life.

Life speaks an eloquent of its own. Our best thoughts comes from others. The thoughts and examples must make sense on their own. If they don't, even a divine footnote cannot provide salvation.

It is not my intention to prescribe behavior or tell you what you should want. Instead, my aim is to illuminate your reality and its opportunities.

Each of us then, within our comfort and belief system, have a way of getting what we want, based on our unique needs. Yes you can!.

Our real world is a giant negotiating table as I said earlier and like it or not, you are a participant. There is always conflict of interest between your families, friends, comrades at work, competitors, the establishments and power structures. How you handle this encounters can determine whether you are to prosper, but you can enjoy a full, pleasurable satisfying life only if you have an independent mind therefore making you sovereign over all.

In fact the biggest question that ever lingers in our mind should be what is it that we really want in life?

Traditionally, rewards presumably go to those possessing the greatest talent, dedication and education. The education of knowing who you are, what you want, and where you are going. But life has illusioned those who hold that virtue and hard work will triumph at the end. The "winners" seem to be people who not only are competent, but also have the ability to "negotiate" their way to get what they want. We negotiate more often than we realize. You must be aware that there are crucial ways to do this for you to succeed:

- Information-this is very important if really you need to be where you want to be. Quite often we fail to realize our dream goals since we even don't know what information is required to get where and what we want. You find that the other people seem to know more about you and your needs than you know about them and their needs. Information is power! So they say. Try as much as possible to gather relevant information regarding what you want and measure whether you are within the scope of your operations. Quite often we make mistakes by trying to measure ourselves with others ahead of us. No! Remember that you are a sovereign and independent person with unique talents and gifts.
- Time- The other people who have always succeeded quite often than not do not find themselves under some kind of organizational pressure, time constraints and restrictive deadlines. But if you have not measured up well with plans, schedules that meet deadlines then definitely you will feel you are under pressure.

This is a situation that may not allow you to succeed because you will always be a failure in not meeting those deadlines. You feel therefore that you are not fit here and there and hence blame games starts. Remember one thing, there is no one ever to prepare plans for you and adequately make sure that you meet the deadlines timely. Take it personally or you become a total failure, a total loser.

- Power-Those who have succeeded in life always seems to have more power and authority than you think you have. Power is a mind blowing entity. It is the capacity or ability to get things done. You must stamp on authority on what you think is right for you. All power is based on perception. If you think you have got it, then you have got it! If you think you don't have it, even if you have it, then you don't have it! In short you have more power if you believe to view life's encounters as negotiations.

Your ability to negotiate determines whether you can or you can't influence your environment. It gives you a sense of mastering over your life. It isn't chiseling and it isn't intimidation of an unsuspecting mark. Its analyzing information, time and power to affect behavior-the meeting of needs (yours and others) to make things happen the way you want them to.

All you need to know is that everything and anything is negotiable. Don't act as though your limited experience represents universal truths. It doesn't. As a negotiator of your own life, take some risk, break free from the precedent of your past experiences of failure, clouds and shadows of fear and self doubt, challenge your assumptions, raise your inspirational level, and increase your expectations.

It is important to note that some things are not the product of a negotiation. It's about common sense. The Ten Commandments was not a negotiated document. It's certainly difficult to negotiate with the Lord when he represents you with a fait accompli etched in stone.

You should always have a sense of mastery over your situation. Pick and choose your opportunities well based upon your needs. Don't compare with others! Always learn to understand what you want and take it personally. Don't allow yourself to be manipulated or intimidated by those who aren't concerned with your best interests. You can play a much greater role than you thought in shaping your life and improving your life style.

Principle 5:

Getting your feet wet

The secret of walking on water is knowing where the stones are! By this I mean you must learn to get involved. Getting involved and as well discovering in the process. In a thousand ways you shall have turned your limitations into beautiful privileges, and enabled you to walk serene and happy in the shadow cast by your deprivation of self doubt and fear in facing life. If you are not prepared to wet your feet, then you should be prepared to know that your life will seem an immense disparity between effort and opportunity. It seems to me that there is in each of us a capacity to comprehend the impressions and emotions which have been experienced by mankind from the beginning. Each individual has a subconscious memory of the green earth and murmuring waters, and blindness and deafness cannot rob him of this gift from the past generations. This inherited capacity is a sort of sixth sense - a soul -sense which sees, hears, feels, all in one.

You should therefore be conscious of a soul-sense that lifts you above the narrow, cramping circumstances of your life. Your physical limitations of self fear, doubt should be forgotten- your world lying upward, the length and the breadth and the sweep of success are all yours!

Principle 6:

Weakness as strength:

In negotiation, dumb is often better than ***Smart.*** Inarticulate frequently better than articulate, and many times weaknesses can actually be ***Strength.*** So train yourself occasionally to say ***"I don't know, I don't understand, you lost me some time ago, or help me,*** when this phrases suit your purposes in life. Admitting that you don't have all the answers humanizes you and causes others to be more receptive to your approach. Don't be a know it all. This hollow, stereotyped model is a ***fraud.*** He's for the birds, because it's self-defeating (and also tiring) to forever stride about, straight backed and dignified, bursting with expertise and knowledge. It's self-defeating to pretend to say the equivalent or I do not know..... help me! Don't be too quick to ***"understand"*** or prove your intellect at the outset of an encounter. Watch your listen-talk ratio. Learn to ask questions even when you think you might know the answers. All you need to do is to make an ultimatum stick.

Principle 7:

The power to be:

Your sovereignty of mind is the transport to your destination but never be a goal in and of itself. The power to implement your plans, the goals is a neutral force like electricity or wind. You need power to protect yourselves and to ensure that you have a sense of mastery of your own lives.

You have that plenty of power. Use it to sensibly implement objectives that are definitely important to you as a person. You indeed own it to yourself not to live by what someone else thinks you ought to do.

When people in our society believe they can't, as individuals, make a difference, it's bad and sad for all of us." Powerless people become a pathetic and toss in the towel, which means others have to carry them on their backs, or they become hostile and try to tear down a system they can't understand and don't believe they can control. This attitude pervades our world. Some of its symptoms are declining productivity and senseless violence.

An example of a person who became violent and hostile is Lynette "Squeaky" Fromme. She attempted to gun down President Gerald Ford. After her arrest, she explained .... "When people around you treat you like a child and pay no attention to the things you say, you have to do ***something.*** The "something" squeaky did was psychopathic and self-destructive. Herself perception was miles off-base. She didn't realize that she had other alternatives that were socially acceptable and legal. She didn't realize that a criminal act, regardless of its goal, is almost always an abuse of power. In essence power is neutral; it's a means, not an end. It's indispensable for mental health & non-aggressive survival and is based upon perception. Within reason, you can get whatever you want if you are aware of your options, if you test your assumptions, if you take shrewdly calculated risks based on solid information, and if you believe you have power.

The formula is laughably that simple. Believe firmly that you have power and you will convey that self-confident perception to others.

It's you who will determine how they see, believe and react to you.

Power like beauty is in the eyes of the beholder....... It begins with you.

Principle 8:

Competition & legitimacy:

Whenever you create competition for something, you possess. What you have moves up in ***value.*** Obviously, the more people who want your money, the further your money will go. Never enter a negotiation without options. If you did, the other person will treat you lightly.

Another source of power at your disposal is the power of legitimacy. In our society people are conditioned to regard with awe anything printed. Printed words, documents, and signs carry authority. Most people tend not to question them. As you negotiate your way through life, legitimacy can be questioned and challenged. Please try and use the power of legitimacy when its advantageous for you to do so.

Alfred P. Doolittle sings: ***In my fair lady:*** *The Lord above made man to help his neighbor no matter where- on land, or sea or foam. But with a little bit of lack, when he comes around, you won't be home.*

To many people this is a competitive world in which ones success is measured not by how well you have done compared to your potential but by how many you have outdistanced. We all live in a society pervaded by potential win-lose situation in which the competitive struggle for admission to a "good college' can be just as rugged as the competition between MacDonald's and Burger

King. Some people interpret this to mean that all life is a constant battle of winning and losing.

They see a world filled with rivals, and competitors, with persons who want their job, their class standing, their money, their promotions, their packing space, their place in line or their spouse.

The competitive negotiator sees almost everything as a constant struggle of winning and losing. In this regard, you need to be a tough battler who seeks to meet own goals at all costs without worrying about the needs and the acceptance of others. There should be no doubt in your mind that you are right in your conviction and approach. If you are such a person, each victory brings a sense of exhilaration.

The competitive (win-lose) approach occurs when someone or some group attempts to achieve their objective at the expense of a perceived adversary. These attempts to triumph over an opponent may ruin the gamut from beautant effort at intimidation to subtle forms of manipulation. This is a self oriented strategy." The soviet style". How do you recognize them? All soviets use the same six steps in their negotiating dance:

- Extreme initial positions:-Always start with tough demands or ridiculous offers that affect the other side's expectation level.
- Limited authority:-The negotiators themselves have little or no authority to make any concessions.
- Emotional tactics:-They get red faced, raise their voices, and act exasperated-horrified that they are being taken advantage of. Occasionally, they will stalk out of a meeting in a huff.
- Adversary Concessions viewed as weakness:-Should you give in and concede them something, they are unlikely to reciprocate.

- Stingy in their concessions:-They delay making any concessions and when they finally do, it reflects only a minuscule change in their position.
- Ignore deadlines:-They tend to be patient and act as though time is of no significance to them. In whichever position you feel you lie you are always right because it's all about you. But remember one thing; that ***"change will not come if we wait for some other person or some other time. We are the ones we have been waiting for. We are the change that we seek"-Barrack Obama (US President).***

Principle 9:

Risk taking:

You must be willing to take risks while negotiating your way through life. Risk taking involves mixing courage with common sense. If you don't take calculated chances or moves, the other people will manipulate you. As Flip Wilson said, ***"before you can hit the jackpot, you have to put a coin in the machine".*** Intelligent risk taking involves knowledge of the ***"ODDS",*** plus a philosophical willingness to shrug your shoulders and absorb a manageable loss without whining. Obviously, the chance of a setback is the price you must pay for any progress. Take risks you can afford without being tight about adverse consequences. In taking risks, you must definitely have a potent force within you, stronger than the persuasion of your friends, stronger than even the pleadings of your heart, which impels you to try your standards of those who have succeeded and failed and tried at the same time. Take optimum or moderate risks.

Don't gamble or "shoot craps with destiny". Before chancing anything, calculate the odds to determine whether the potential benefits are worth the possible cost of failure. Be rational, not impulsive. Never take a risk out of pride, impatience or a desire to get it over with.

Principle 10:

Commitment:

Don't crawl out on a limb that might be served off, to become either a hero today or a zero tomorrow. Persuade others to help, get them involved in the planning and decision making and they will shoulder part of the blunder. Remember people support that which they help to create. The application of the power of commitment can work in three ways:

1. By disposing the overall risk, you can take advantage of propitious circumstances.
2. Since your associates share the total anxiety and lend their support, your stress levels will definitely reduce.
3. The shoulder to shoulder dedication of your group transmits awesome power vibrations to other people.

In fact, involvement begets commitment -commitment begets power. You need not to fake your capacity because you have much more potential than you think.

Principle 11:

Expertise and knowledge:

When others perceive or believe that you have more technical knowledge, specialized skill, or experience than you have, they treat you with a consideration that ranges from respect to awe. Don't be pretentious.

In today's world where knowledge keeps about as well as dead fish (and even under refrigeration that's not so long) it's impossible to be an expertise in all areas. Knowledge of needs must be bargained as well. The specific issues and demands which are stated openly, the real needs of the other people which are really verbalized. This knowledge first must come from the self. For after all, everyone who wishes to gain true knowledge of the self must climb the hill difficulty alone, and since there is no royal road to the summit, you must zigzag it in your own way. Remember that you will slip back many times, you will fall, and you will at times need to stand still, running against the edge of hidden obstacles. You will at times lose your tempers and find it again and keep it better. All you need to do friend /brother/sister, is to trudge on, gain a little, feel encouraged, get more eager and climb higher and begin to see the widening horizon. Every struggle is victory. One more effort and you reach the luminous cloud, the blue depths of the sky, the uplands of your desire. You are not always alone however; in this struggles.

Isaiah's prophecy should be fulfilled in you. ***" The mountains and the hills shall break forth before you into singing, and all the trees of the field shall clap their hands!"***

Principle 12:

Investment:

It's important as an independent sovereign person to invest in time, money or energy towards the achievement of goals. This will give you more tact for tomorrow. Day in day out, life becomes a huddle to cross over to the other side of success all for want of tact. This subtle, highly desirable quality is the very lubricant of living. With it the wheels of life turn smoothly; without it all is discord and fiction.

The tactless person leaves a trail of wounded spirits. Life offers a thousand situations where a little tact will act as oil in machinery. For instance, it is tactful to be investment conscious for from it you will advance in terms of wealth creation. Man is disturbed by circumstances as long as he believes himself to be a creature of outside conditions, but when he realizes that he is a creative power and he can command the hidden soil and seeds of his being out of which circumstances grow he becomes the rightful master of himself. It is therefore of paramount importance to realize that tapping your potential geared towards investment requires the understanding of your subconscious mind, willpower and the action of the heart and the sincere desire to serve the world.

Your life is in your hands. The decision, choice to use and follow your intuition lies with you.

Principle 13:

Identification:

You will need to maximize your negotiating ability if you get others identify with you. The power of identification exists in all interpersonal relationships, business transactions & even politics. We are all influenced by those with whom we can identify. More often people care to admit, identification whether with or against plays a significant role in negotiations & decision making. That is why behaving decently and trying to help others is equivalent of having a canteen of water in the Gobi Desert.

Principle 13:

Precedent:

Don't act as though your limited experience represents universal truths. Force yourself to go outside your experience by testing your assumptions. Don't lock yourself into time-worn ways of doing things. It is easy to lock yourself-in or to get locked in by others-because one aspect of the power of precedent is based on a "don't make waves", "you can't argue with success" and "we have always done it this way outlook". In other words if people at point A do something and people at point B learn about it, it affects the way people at point B act. Information spreads fast to justify what you are doing or asking for, always refer to other situations similar to the one you are currently in, where you or others did so and so, and the result you wanted occurred.

Principle 14:

Persistence:

Persistence is to power what carbon is to steel. Learn to hang in there. You must be tenacious. We are told that; that was an admirable quality president Jimmy Carter had. He was tenacious. He was steadfast and remarkably persistent. Persistence pays off. Persistence is so key to your success in life that genius, talents, gifts do not guarantee you success. Only persistence does. ***"Our ideals resemble the stars, which illuminate the night. No one will ever be able to touch them. But the ones, who like the sailors on the ocean, take them for guides, will undoubtedly reach their goal".*** This is persistence no doubt! The meek shall inherit the Earth- but not its mineral rights said J. Paul Getty.

"Christopher Columbus went on an expedition to find the shortest route to India from Europe. His crew grew anxious as they sailed further away from home. Some threatened to mutiny and demanded that he turn back. He finally asked for fourty eight hours more at the end of which, he said, the sailors could kill him if they had not reached America. The rest, as they say, is history. Columbus goal to achieve the objective was so firm that it created in him a great desire and stay in power even in the face of setbacks".

As you read this book I think your journey has began if ever you have never been persistent in life. ***" If you want to be happy, set a goal that commands your thoughts, liberates your energy, and inspires your hope" (Andreaw Carnegie).***

Principle 15:

Capacity:

Most of us in the civilized society rely too heavily on reasoning capacity to make things happen. We have been raised to believe that logic will prevail. Logic in and of itself, will rarely influence people. Most often logic doesn't work. In convincing and making one belief in something you must rely on three (3) things:

- To be understood what you are saying. You must enter someone's world. Something that relates to one's experience.
- Your evidence to be so overwhelming that it can't be disputed.
- Ones believing must meet your existing needs and desires.

Is it that the sun revolves around the earth or the earth revolves around the sun? If you want to persuade people, show the immediate relevance and value of what you are saying in terms of meeting their needs and desires.

Principle 16:

Attitude:

Whose the worst person you can negotiate for? ***Yourself.*** You do a much better job negotiating for someone else. ***Why...***because you take yourself so seriously in any interaction that concerns you. You care too much about yourself. Try to regard all encounters and situations, including your job, as a game, as the world of illusion. Pull back a little and enjoy it all. Do your best, but don't fall apart if everything doesn't pass out the way you would like it to. Remember that things are seldom what they seem.

If you develop this healthy game of attitude in all your negotiation encounters, both on and off the job, three benefits will follow:

- You will have considerably more energy because you will always have energy to do the things you enjoy doing.
- You will be under reduced stress. There will be less uric acid in your blood stream, and the tendency towards hypertension will diminish.
- You will get better results, because your attitude will convey your feeling of power and mastery of your life. (You will transmit a confidence indicative of options, and people will start following you).

Principle 17:

Mutual satisfaction:

Hold it! I really don't care who cuts the pie into two pieces, but whoever does has to give the other the right to select the piece they want. There are many situations in which the needs of the protagonists are not really in opposition. If the focus shifts from defeating each other to defeating the problem, everyone can benefit.

In collaborative **win-win** negotiation we are trying to produce an outcome that provides acceptance gain to all parties. Conflict is regarded as a natural part of the human condition. If conflict is viewed as a problem to be solved, creative solutions can be found that enhance the position of both sides and the parties may even be brought closer together.

Since nature does not create all human beings alike. Your needs & my needs are usually not identical. Therefore, it's possible for both of us to emerge victorious. How?

Using the process to meet needs: - at the outset of negotiating, you should always come on like velvet, not coarse sand paper. State your case moderately, scratch your head, and admit you might even be in error. Remember to err is human; forgive, divine. Don't hesitate to say I need your help with this problem, because I don't know. Everything is in the approach.

Harmonizing or reconciling needs: - Unfortunately when people see themselves as adversaries they deal at arm's length or even through third parties. From this distance they state demands and counter demands, pronounce conditions, and hurl ultimatums at each other. Obviously in such a climate, it is virtually impossible to negotiate for the satisfaction of mutual needs. This needs free interaction and sharing creative solutions that eventually may lead to both sides as winners. Acting as collaborators, they come up with a creative solution to their problem that satisfies them both. You should always remember that conflict may not be missing in this process. Conflict is an unavoidable part of life. Some of us have goals that are in opposition. But conflicts, no matter what its form - from the disposition of a slab of pie to the distribution of a million dollars-will often rise even if both sides are in agreement on what they want.

The reason we are at odds on an issue may stem from three areas of difference:

- **Experience:** - You and I do not see things as they are. Clearly each person is the product of his or her experience and no two people can have identical imprinting. ***" We are all captives of the pictures in our head-our beliefs that the world we have experienced is the world that exists"*** *Journalist Walter Lippman.*

To understand how one thinks & interpret events, we must get into their world. To fathom their behavior, we must try to elicit their feelings, attitudes and belief system.

- **Information**:-Obviously, if we are working from a different information base, we will end up poles apart. If an approaching conflict is to be minimized, we must be willing to share this knowledge with each other.
- **Role**: - Very often divergent views are a result of the part you have been given to play in the negotiation drama. The role or job you have affects how you perceive the situation and colors your view of what might constitute an equitable settlement. Overall therefore, the emphasis is not upon slick maneuvers that finesse or manipulate the other side, rather, its on the development of genuine relationships based upon trust, where both sides win. Successful collaborative negotiation lies in finding out what the other side really wants and showing them a way to get it, while you get what you want.

"It is not over until it's over"-Yogi Bera. Accomplishing mutual satisfaction using the collaborative ***win-win*** style involves emphasis on three important activities:

1. **Building trust**: - In a continuing relationship, the more trust you place in others, the more they will justify your faith. Convey your belief in their honesty and reliability and you will encourage them to live up to these expectations. What is the alternative? Stamp out suspicions and distrust and surely you will have a prophecy fulfilled.

Thus the only way to save ourselves from the worst may just be to expect the best. The best is a trusting relationship, in which each party has a firm belief in the honesty and reliability of the other. It is mutual dependence - a potential alliance to deal with inevitable disagreement. It is a climate that lays the foundation for transforming conflict into satisfying outcomes. This mutual trust is the main spring of collaborative **win-win** negotiations. Activity of building trust is two-fold:

a). The process stage- Building trusted relationships-"Our world may be one of the walking paranoia but trust is the universal lubricant".

b). The formal event-Once a relationship of trust has been established, it elicits recognition of mutual vulnerability. It prevents disruptive conflict from developing, and it encourages the sharing of information.

2. **Gaining commitment**: - No individual is an isolated entity. Everyone that you deal with is being reinforced by those around them. You may be the hub or core, but the bodies rotating about you influence your behavior. ***" Things are in the saddle and they ride mankind"***said Emerson. Never see any one as an isolated unit. See those whom you wish to persuade in context, as a central core around which others move. Get the support of those others and you will influence the position and movement of the core.

3. **Dealing with opposition:-** To progress to your place in the sun, you must always put up with some blisters, those who dispute your right of passage. There is nothing wrong in having this opposition. From it, you sharpen your mind, increase your skill, and add zest to your life. In fair competition with an opponent you gain insight into yourself that will foster growth & development. As Walt Whiteman once wrote," ***Have you not learned great lessons from those who braced themselves against you?"*** Opposition is what life is all about. Your entire muscular system depends on it. When an infant first tries to stand, he encounters resistance from the force of gravity and falls down. But as he persists, he builds the muscles in his arms, legs and back until he finally rises. Dealing with opposition can keep you alert. To get what you want, you have to encounter opposition. If you have no opponents, it may be that you are still seated. In essence, you are not negotiating to get the result you want provided that you are doing nothing, you will soon get opponents. ***From whence cometh opposition?*** Opposition comes in two fold:-

a). Idea opponents:- An idea opponent is one who disagrees with you on a particular issue or alternative. The disparity of misunderstanding is theoretical. ***" I think it should be done this way".*** This method encourages the pooling of ideas, information, experience and feelings to find a mutually beneficial outcome.

It is even possible, with both sides working together, to bring about a synergistic result. This happens when the final result surpasses the contributions of both sides. Where synergy occurs, the whole is greater than the sum of its parts. When this occurs, you used the pressure of adversity or opposition to help you get what you want. In this way an idea opponent is always a potential ally.

b). Visceral opponents: - Is an emotional adversary who not only disagrees with your point of view but disagrees with you as a human being. Once you make visceral opponents, they tend to stay with you for a long time, for they are difficult to convert. So try not to bring them into being in the first place.

Avoid providing a visceral opponent the way you would avoid a contagious disease. ***"For every action there is a reaction".*** The gist of this was verbalized by Bernard Barach when he said ***"Two things are bad for the heart-running up stairs and running down people".*** Ultimately, the avoidance of visceral opposition is the avoidance of mutual dissatisfaction.

In order not to make visceral opponents, you need do the following:

1. Never forget the power of your attitude: - Negotiation is a game- ***"Care, but don't care that much".*** Even if you have a just cause to retaliate, restrain yourself. Remember, the provocative act by itself rarely upsets you; no one and nothing can irritate you without your consent.

Thomas Jefferson was alluding to this demeanor when he said ***"Nothing gives a person so much advantage over another as to remain always cool and unruffled under all circumstances".***

2. **Never judge the actions and motives of others: -** Since you cannot look into someone's heart or mind, it would seem absurd to believe that you might know what impels or propels them. Many times they even don't know. Note that you cannot get what you want if you recognize that each person is unique and needs can be reconciled. At the same time never forget that most needs can be fulfilled by the way you act and behave. Mutual satisfaction should be your goal and the means of achieving-collaborative ***win-win*** negotiations.

What I'm saying is that you have the power to negotiate anything at any place anywhere as long as you have the sovereignty of mind. Indeed you are the power figure! ***" He is free who knows how to keep in his own hands the power to decide-*** said Salvador de Madriaga.In any type of negotiation, quick is always synonymous with risk- undue haste puts one party in jeopardy. If you don't know where you are going, when you get there, you don't even know you are there! ***"Nothing will happen until you make it happen! Who can better interpret the chicken scratches than the chicken that scratched them?***

To hold your audience, you must make the bible come alive. Your flock must see those times and events as if they were happening today. Remember Jesus interest was in the redemption of man's very humanity. His mission was not to

govern men, but to release them." OH! Yes. It might help you relax a little if you put some VODKA or GIN in your water glass".

Chapter three:

Acres of diamond:

It was first developed just after the American civil war in form of a lecture entitled ***'Acres of diamond'*** by a lawyer and newspaper editor named **Russell H. Conwell.**

In 1881, Dr. Conwell also became a church minister and it was in this role that he developed his talk, which he delivered some **8,000 times** to audiences across America. These public talks earned him **$ 8 million** (equivalent to our 600 million shillings) in lecture fees, which he used to found his Temple University in Philadelphia, Pennsylvania, to serve **"the poor but deserving men."**

"Acres of diamond" was the true story of a poor farmer who settled in Africa and spent years struggling to raise his crops. His land was difficult and rocky to till. Disturbed with his circumstances, the farmer became increasingly fascinated by tales of **"easy wealth"** attained by men who had searched for and discovered diamonds in the country side. He too wanted to be rich. He grew tired of the endless labor and impulsively sold his farm to search for diamonds. For the rest of his life he wondered the vast African continent searching for the gleaning gems. But the great discovery eluded him. Finally in a fit of despondency, broken financially, he threw himself into the river and drowned.

Meanwhile the man who had bought his farm found a large and unusual stone in a stream that cut through his land. It turned out to be a diamond of enormous value.

Stunned by his new found wealth, the farmer discovered that his land was virtually covered with such stones. It was to become one of the world's richest diamond mines.

Now the first farmer had unknowingly owned acres of diamonds. He sold it practically for nothing in order to look for riches elsewhere. If only he had taken time **to study** and realize what diamonds look like in their rough state, and had first **thoroughly explored the land he owned,** he would have found riches he sought - on the land he had been living on.

What so affected Dr. Conwell and subsequently thousands of others who had this lecture, was the fact that each one of us, at any moment, is standing on the middle of his/her **own acres of diamonds**.

If only we acquire the wisdom and the patience to intelligently and effectively explore our life, lifting our weights inside out, we will definitely find that it contains the riches we seek- whether they are material, spiritual or both.

Before we go running off to what we think are greener pastures, let's make sure that our own is not as green, or perhaps even greener. Often times, while we are looking at other pastures (jobs, business etc), other people are busy looking at ours. There is nothing pitiful than the person who wastes his/her life wandering from one thing to another, like the improvident seeker of the diamonds, forever looking for the pot of gold at the end of the rainbow and never staying with one thing long enough to find it.

For no matter what your goals may be, or whatsoever form your riches may take, you can be sure that your start on the **road to its attainment** can be found somewhere within your **present surroundings**. And that is the road map I would like to share with you in this book.

Key issues:

- The key to having the life you want is inside you; you already have what it takes to get what you want. What is inside each of us is powerful enough to help us achieve anything we want.
- You are what you think you are. As a man thinketh so he is!
- People are always blaming circumstances for what they are. Don't believe in circumstances. The people who get on in this world are people who get up and look for the circumstances they want, and if they can't find them, make them.
- If you bring forth what is within you, what you bring forth will save you. If you do not bring forth what is within you, what you do not bring forth will destroy you.
- Your life mission is the north point in your personal compass.
  Use it to guide you in your life decisions.
  I have written my life in small sketches, a little today, a little yesterday......
  I look back on my life as good day's work it was done and I feel satisfied with it.
  I made the best out of what life offered. -*Anna Mary Robertson.*

Look at your life and see what assets and passions you have for your own personal fulfillment in the process; you will also enrich the world.

Topic 1:

Discovering yourself:

Self discovery is a matter of **self analysis and application**.

The moment you let the opinion of others control your life is the moment you lose your uniqueness, the special quality that makes you.

The following questions should be critically analyzed:

- Where are you now in this journey of life?
- What drives you?-Every human being is driven by something.
- Are you driven by your peer group?
- Do you ask yourself what other people will think when you do something?
- Are you driven by fear, anger, guilt, greed or your past?
- Are you driven by your spouse?

There is no greater goal and more fulfilling objective than to discover and do your purpose in life. Allow these to be your driving force and pursue it with passion.

The tragedy of life is that most people go their entire lives without ever learning what their purpose is, never discovering their niche(strengths and special advantage areas), never finding the place where they fit.

Most of us live on the survival level where we barely eke out a life. We are merely existing and not really enjoying life. We put our hope on month end pay Cheque.

We just exist and vegetate. **Where are you? Are you smart, talented and still struggling with life? Are you a qualified professional and still struggling with life?**

Are you hard working person but still struggling with life?

The best way out is for you to meditate upon your personal potential mix here under in order for you to discover your unique placing in the universe.

Abilities → Talents, Gifts, Skills

Exposure→ Cultural programming-social and life experiences.

Personality→ Genetic programming unique to you.

The above once appreciated will lead you to benefits of self discovery and hence self leadership. This means that you need to focus on what you are good at. It will also help you build a life's foundation on your potential and standing out as a wealth creator and hence a person of significance.

Personality: "We come to love not by finding a perfect person, but by learning to see an imperfect person perfectly". A person's behavior is far from random. We have preferences of how we approach life, how we get energized, how we take information, and how we make decisions and orient ourselves to life. If we chose tasks, work settings or occupations that are not a good fit for your personality, you may end up feeling tired and discouraged.

Exposure: This entails appreciating your life's cultural programming both socially and experiences you have gone through. This is in line with the education system, the type of family, the community and the work environment that you have been exposed to.

These constitute your reaction to events in your life and they then contribute to the choices you make in life.

Talents, Gifts and Skills: ***"Mediocrity knows nothing higher than self, but talent instantly recognizes genius". -Arthur Doyle, Snr.***

Naturally recurring behaviors and feelings constitute your talent, gifts and skills.

You must discover the essential "you" the person who truly resides behind the facades, defenses and stresses of every day life.

Once unmasked you put yourself in the best position to live your life and enjoy it.

Questions to ponder & explore:

1. ***When have you been most committed, passionate and enthusiastic?***
2. ***When have you been most creative?***
3. ***When have you been sure of yourself and your decisions?***
4. ***What do your consider to be your greatest accomplishments?***
5. ***When have other people considered you most successful?***
6. ***When have you enjoyed your work the most?***
7. ***What talents were you relying on and using in these situations?***
8. ***For what would you make a strong stand for?***
9. ***What in the world disturbs you and you feel you can make an impact on?***

10. ***What activities are you drawn towards?***

11. ***If money were no concern, what would you be doing?***

Brainstorm these questions and use them to identify the top three talents you mostly use when you are most successful. Answers to these questions will bring you towards understanding your value in any work environment.

Soul (mind, will and emotions):

The mind refers to the aspects of intellect and consciousness manifested as combinations of thought, perception, memory and emotion. The mind constitutes the thinking brain and the feeling brain which work together.

Body (health):

This is the vehicle that takes you towards your destiny. It must be properly managed and frequently serviced in order for it to create wealth in your life.

Spiritual (intuition):

It is important to acknowledge that you are a spiritual being having human experiences. Connecting to your spirit means connecting to the captain of your ship, which will take you to your ordained destination.

Topic 1 (ii):

Self discovery-Defined:

Is the act or purpose of achieving understanding or knowledge of oneself. The ideal of self understanding is as old as the great age of classical Greece evidenced by the injunction "know thyself" and the statement- ***'The unexamined life is not worth living.'***

In human existence, a question commonly asked is **'WHO AM I?'**. This question is the HEART of the quest for SELF. This is a quest which may take a life time, sometimes longer to fulfill.

However, what is important is that you must create your life **"inside out"**. What were you born to be? What is your purpose for living? Are you doing the things you love doing?

Do you love your work? Or if you are not working what would you love to do? What is your passion? What drives you most?

Note that people who are in touch with their authentic self **(True)** have no boundaries between work and play. It is fan to work. They have passion for their work.

Examples:

1. Public speaker: Who is passing an important message-social, health; environment issues may do so with excitement, zeal and joy because it is his love/passion.
2. A teacher who cultivates his students and causes their eager minds to learn with joy and excitement is in love with his work and enjoys.

The art of self discovery:

One path of self discovery is

1. When people turn their surroundings in their search. In turning to their surroundings, people are able to see their selves by the things around them. In observing the surroundings, people may not only find their selves, but establish their selves. The path, however, is not the only way people search for the self.
2. Another path is when people turn something higher than themselves for answers. This path is lined with the hope that answers can be given by the "something higher". These two paths represent two preceding forces in people's search for self.

The two forces are absolute and the other. The absolute is something higher, (a sage-self or higher self).This is a part of our psyche that is much wiser than the rest of us, much more in contact with our deepest needs and best possibilities. It is a powerful metaphor and perhaps a bit more than a metaphor.

All of us have known moments of extraordinary lucidity when ordinary limitations and constraints seem to fall away. We can then look objectively with almost supernormal clarity. That perspective is called sage-self. This is a state of consciousness and this is the stage that as human beings, are transformed. At this stage, there is a higher order of consciousness, almost as a preview of the next stage of our evolution.

The other presents people the self comes in contact with. Only through interaction and contact with the absolute and the other, can the self discover itself. In the interaction with these two forces, a balance must exist. The balance allows for the contact with the absolute, and the interaction with the other, to complement and enhance each other.

In Marie Von Ebners novel -Das Gemeinderkind she displays the necessity for the relationship between the self, the absolute, and the other in search for the self.

Factors/Attributes hindering self discovery:

The issue of self-esteem is perhaps one of the greatest determinates in creating a life of freedom and abundance, or feeling inhibited and "just getting by". Self-esteem is defined as "a feeling of pride in oneself". It is how you feel in relation to yourself rather than how others see you. It's between you and, well you. Therefore, its not necessary to be so concerned about what others think to determine your level of self -esteem, as the definition does not include any "others", just you. So where can you help yourself to better understand you? There are so many aspects of you but one that is of great importance is that of your mind.

In the ancient wisdom of Patanjalis Yoga Sutras, there are five hindrances or afflictions of the mind that are collectively known as the klesas. An understanding of each of these hindrances can help play a part in the discovery of self, leading to a feeling of well-being, connectivity , and greater self-esteem.

The hindrances are as follows: ignorance ,egoism, attachment aversion and clinging to life. Encountering the afflictions without being aware of them creates stumbling blocks on the path to self-realization. The afflictions will arise at different times in life, but if one has spent time studying them, one may be able to recognize them for what they are and move through them with a certain level of personal understanding.

The first hindrance is ignorance of the true self which is the building block for all of the other afflictions. It can be described as an incorrect understanding of oneself that is the culmination of years of unconscious actions, thoughts, and words that one has become dependent upon as part of ones being. Sound familiar? How many times have we replayed old tapes over and over in our head until they become so embedded in our persona that we begin to self-realize these false beliefs? From ignorance, derives judgments of oneself and of others. By understanding the various afflictions and where they originate, one may transcend a lifetime absorbed in ignorance.

The second hindrance is egoism which is the identification of the self with what one is not- the body, mind, personality, emotions, senses, accomplishments, failures, and possessions, or lack thereof. You may be thinking, "People with low self-esteem are certainly not showing an ego problem." Well, it actually is an ego problem, as the concern over what others think dominates many choices and actions in daily life. In egoism, the practice of remaining in the moment and being a non-judgmental witness comes in handy. In truly observing what is happening in life as it is, rather than placing violent judgments on self, others and situations, one may experience life with a limited ignorance. Imagine viewing the world through a camera lens and just seeing what is-nothing else.

The third hindrance is attachment which arises from the egos idea that more is better and of the fear of losing what one already has in his/her possession. Are you keeping up with the Jones? Do you really need to be? More stuff just means more upkeep; right? As one progresses on the life path, experiences occur that cause feelings of great pleasure.

One may cling to these things in hopes of experiencing the feelings over and over again. Attachment is looking outside of oneself for validation and bliss. The reality is that external factors come and go; it is the internal true self that remains a constant. "Happiness is found within", is a timeless phrase and it is unconditional and independent of any outside circumstances or people. Freeing, isn't it?

The fourth hindrance is aversion which is also a form of attachment, but in the negative sense. The experiences or circumstances that one does not want to have, or is repulsed by, comprise aversions. Aversions are typically based on fear of the unknown, unfamiliar, or years of subconscious mechanical thought. Fear plays a big role in issues of low self-esteem. Attachments and aversions are both relative in that what is a good/bad experience or feeling for one may not be so good/bad for another. Any attachment or aversion springs from the imagination and can be construed as clinging, and therefore, in turn, suffering. By practicing detachment to either aversions or attachments, one can see a situation for what it is rather than what it is perceived to be.

Clinging to life or the fear of death is the final hindrance. It is self-preservation and the fundamental will to live in ones body on this Earth. This affliction is said to be experienced even by the very wise. It is ultimately the understanding of this affliction that will set us free. Each individual would come to terms with this hindrance by their own accord in relation to their own belief system regarding death and what happens when we leave our physical body. It is my sense that we are eternal in spirit.

The klesas are complex and interwoven. By increasing the understanding of each affliction, one may begin to identify them when they surface in life. In knowing where the reaction, situation, or behavior is derived, the individual may be better able to experience the true sense of the moment in awareness and without judgment. By remaining open, one is able to receive the perfection in every moment.

It is a daily process to connect with oneself in understanding, but one that can create a life that is, for the most part, joyous, peaceful, and full of love. With practice the sense of self-esteem will continuously improve and the feelings of a life connectedness will deepen. Try it for yourself as this all begins and ends with you. For, it's what you think that really matters. ***"The mind is everything; what you think, you become." (Buddha)***

Attributes for self discovery:

All that you accomplish or fail to accomplish with your life is the direct result of your thoughts-James Allen.

1) First, **transform your thoughts into reality:** Identify your inner calling viz a viz potential. You are literally what you think and your character is the complete sum of all your thoughts. In other words what you are thinking now, tomorrow and the next month, is what you will eventually become. What is it that you really/truly seek from life? "Man is made or unmade by himself; in the armory of thought, he forges the weapons by which he destroys himself; he also fashions the tools by which he builds for himself heavenly mansions of joy and strength and peace.

2) Commitment to reinforce the potential for proper manifestation:

The self discovery will grow from seeds of THOUGHT, seeds that only you can plant now that you understand this great truth and the control you have over your destiny.

Thus; you are the designer of your destiny

You are the author

You are the story

The pen is in your hands

The outcome is whatever you choose.

3). Visions & ideals: The dreamers are the saviors of the world. As the visible world is sustained by the invisible, so man, through their trials and sins and sordid vocations, are nourished by the beautiful visions of their solitary dreamers. Humanity cannot forget its dreamers; it cannot let their ideals fade and die; it leaves in them; it knows them as the realities which it shall one day see and know.

He who cherishes a beautiful vision, a lofty ideal in his heart, will one day realize it.

Columbus cherished a vision of another world, and he discovered it; Corpnicus fostered the vision of a multiplicity of worlds and a wider universe, and he revealed it; Buddha beheld the vision of a spiritual world of stainless beauty and perfect peace and he entered into it.

Cherish your visions; cherish your ideals, cherish the music that stirs in your heart, the beauty that forms in your mind, the loveliness that drapes your purest thoughts, for out of them will grow all delightful conditions, all heavenly environment; of these if you but remain true to them, your world will at last be built. Your vision is the promise of what you shall one day be; your ideal is the prophecy of what you shall at last unveil'. Dreams are the seedlings of realities.

4).Look for opportunities: Look for opportunities which fit the scope of your expanding powers.

The vision that you glorify in your mind, the ideal that you enthrone in your heart-This you will build your life by, this you will become. Be serious to developing your strength to seize opportunities.

'You may live in an imperfect world but the frontiers are not closed and the doors are not all shut'-Dr.Maxwell Maltz.

5). Raising self esteem and developing self confidence: You are an extremely valuable, worthwhile, significant person even though your present circumstances may have you feeling otherwise. Through this you can win your war against negative feelings. Your life need not be a succession of 24 hour vacuums, nor must you live in an emotional dungeon any longer.

6). Find the courage to take risks: How much of your talent is being wasted for want of little boldness? Whatever you think you will eventually become.......... And you do have all the POTENTIAL! People don't change when they feel good. They change when they are fed up.

When things are going all right, we all tend to do pretty much what we have been doing. Pain pushes us to those crucial turning points-When hurt, then finally choose. It's that adverb, finally -Enough is enough.

7). Attract success- To attract success and in wanting to be successful, there are three things:

- **Know what you are doing**
- **Love what you are doing**
- **And believe in what you are doing.**

Success today is a journey and not a destination. And in making this trip the most important thing is that we must be constantly moving forward. Yes-the progressive realization of pre-determined goal. And our growth should never end. Any person, who selects a goal in life which can be fully achieved, has already defined his own limitations. Note that when we cease to grow, we begin to die.

8). Taking charge of one's life: You have only one life. Are you living it with self respect, with purpose, with a strategy for continued growth- or are you little more than a live marionette with others pulling your strings? As Jules Henry, the anthropologist, has commented; *'he is a creative external to himself, a surface of fear moved by the winds of circumstance: once circumstance colliding with another-that is the ebb and flow thought or he is a cyclone of fear in which impulses from the outer world collide at random"* When we live a life of sham Henry goes on by saying that we do not consider reality- but only try to defeat it.

9).Look like a winner-' ***The image you project in many circumstances, is far more valuable than your skills or your record of past accomplishments'***-Michael Korda.

What do people see when they glance in your direction? An obvious success? Or a more obvious loser in life? And by what means, what value system, do they dare pass on you, a stranger in some cases, so swiftly? You already know the answer: **By how you look!**

Daniel Webster was correct when he said ***"The world is governed more by appearances than realities".***

10).Learn to swap a losing strategy: 'There are many ways you can get out of the ruts of boredom and mediocrity before you run out of road'.-*Auren Uris & Jack Tarrant.*

Topic 2:

Principles of success:-key issues:

1. You must believe in yourself, have faith in yourself and have confidence in yourself. In short, you must be totally **aware of your own self worth (Value).**
2. There is only one you. There is no one in the entire world to equal you, to match your finger prints or to match your voice, to match your features or to match your personality. You are an original in the fullest sense of the word. You are number one. And now that you know it, **your job is to reinforce that fact in your conscious and subconscious mind every day**. All you need to know is that 95% of all human problems stem from a negative mind. Getting successful and rich is universal. **Remember that you possess not only things money can buy, but also the deep inward satisfaction that comes with making life what you want it to be.**
3. There are three kinds of people:
    - **Achievers**:-They are always enthused, they never complain, they wear a number one smile. They are positive proof **that what they get out of life is what you put into it. They are winners**. And they have the ability to charge your battery with their enthusiasm. **Those are the people you want to emulate**.

- They are the people who are always looking for a shoulder to cry on, for someone to tell their troubles to. They are the **Grippers** in life. They are **put-downers** and **pull-downers.** They are **losers,** the people to stay away from. Run from them to avoid any danger of becoming like them.
- They are the people who have **cooped-out** of life, who have simply **given-up**. Their attitude is **"What's the use?** They are the ones who say **"Let George do it"**. In a way they are even more pitiful losers than the number twos because **they have never made an effort -SHUN THEM!**

4. **The road to winning / succeeding:**

   You can only win in any business geared towards success by believing you are number one and acting like it. By reminding yourself every day-verbally or some visible sign-that you are number one. Just as plants need fertilizing, so does your mind. If you want a winning image with others, your first concern must be a **winning self -image**.

5. **The most powerful words in the world:**

   Dr.Norman Vincent Pearle said that there are two most powerful words in the world. The first has only five letters, but it has the strength to move mountains.

That word is called **Faith-**Faith in yourself, faith in others, faith in your abilities, faith in today, and faith in your future. **If you don't have it, who will have it for you?** The second has four letters-**Fear-**Fear that you cant be, that you cant belong, or do something, fear of the past and its consequences, fear of tomorrow for what tomorrow might bring, fear that you might fail.

6. **Note:** That confidence breeds confidence. There are five rules to get rid of fear. They will help you to banish out fear and replace it with confidence and courage.
    i. **Believe in yourself-**Self confidence starts with belief in yourself. Seven words to remember-**You can if you think you can.**
    ii. **Associate with confident people-**Stay away from negative, fearful people-Confidence breeds confidence.
    iii. **Tune up your confidence machine:-**Clean up your carburetor of your confidence machine with additive faith. Your confidence machine will only keep working if you keep it cleaned, fueled, oiled & finely tuned.

iv. **Be the master/captain of your own ship**: Henry Ford said that all confident & successful people gained their courage by facing their fears instead of running away from them. Face yourself doubts squarely & say **am i bigger than they are or are they bigger than i?-Be the captain of your ship.**

v. **Keep busy-**In a busy person fear and self - doubt can find little room to dwell. James K. Van Fleet counsels in his book **Miracle People Power- To act as if it were impossible to fail and do the thing you fear to do. Go to it! Go for it!**

7. Success such a magical word-It creates enticing visions in the minds of all of us. **Has it been missing in your life?** Even if it has, **you still day dream don't you?** About how things might be if only fate would smile in your direction & bestow upon you a more generous portion if your money, position, power, freedom,& perhaps even a touch of fame?
8. **Why is success so difficult?**
   - We are each of us a miracle we are told.
   - We all engage ourselves in dreams and wishes: **To be free from want, to live a finer home etc-Why then is success difficult? Aren't we in a land of unlimited opportunity?** The vast majority of us have no idea how to begin to make our dreams come true. We have all the tools necessary to do this.

But what good are they if you don't know how to use them? Can we build a life worth living without any plans or blue prints? Is it too late for you to reach for the bras ring or make a run for the roses? Should you crawl into a dusty little corner of self-pity & just let the world pass you by? No never, you have the **Potential---- The gold mine is within you...... go...... go......for it!**

Topic 3:

Key principles to wealth creation:

What's the plan for your future? Is it short term or long term?

What do you have that you are not using?

"If we had no winter, the spring would not be so pleasant; if we did not sometimes have a taste of adversity, prosperity would not be so welcome" Anne Bradstreet once said"-We are told a fool and his money are soon parted. This means that a fool doesn't know how to manage the wealth creation process. A fool has a consumption mind set that is, spending on things that do not create value addition.

For you to create wealth in your life it is important for you to have fundamental shift of mind and to start seeing things in a different way:

1. **Your money is yours, when**......Count your money after you have paid or taken in consideration all the bills, taxes and the current inflation rate. This will help you to appreciate your real value at a specific point in time. Whenever financial decision you will make there after will be based on your true financial position.
2. **Make a maximum use of all your assets**-Our existing assets include all our human, intellectual, financial and civic assets. Spend time with yourself. Brainstorm and meditate on all the assets you have because, maximizing on these promises you are a fun-filled wealthy life.

   Sacrifice to invest in things which go up in value.

3. **Concentrate your investment on areas that you fully understand:-** Pick strong investments, understand them fully and throw your whole energy into them. We fail to create wealth simply because we so much dwell on what we don't know either through poor research or by sheer lack following other people's footsteps and dreams that are not entirely our own.
4. **Be aggressive and chase for opportunities:-**A wise wealth seeker is always on the offensive, always a learner, always on the look out for opportunities and maximizing them. ***Avoid the tendency to preserve and protect because your assets will not grow. Instead, be a risk taker.***
5. **Ascertain that your wealth grows on a wealth producing rate of return:-**wise debt management can buy you a life time that is debt free. Debt can be an effective way to increase your net-wealth if used for the right purposes in the right way. Borrowing money to buy assets which will continue to produce income can be considered "good debt" because it has the ability to increase your net wealth overtime, and help you towards a financial secure future.
6. **There is no perfect investment:-**Appreciate that there is no such a thing as perfect investment. Just make sure your investment is the one that grows surely, steadily and relentlessly upward in value without a lot of fluctuations.

7. **Control**:-People lose their money mostly by transferring ultimate control of their financial decision making to someone else. Through outright stealing, ineptitude, bad lack or a mixture of all these , the investment goes down the drain. It is critical to create systems of control for any investment you undertake. ***Be in a position to appreciate at what stage of wealth creation your investment is in.***
8. **Develop a wealth mind set**:-Note that your expectations dictate how the world works or ought to work around you. The way you view the world creates your reality. ***As a man thinketh so he is……If you think you are right or wrong, you are always right-Henry Ford. The only way you can loosen your outdated assumptions is to know where they came from.*** It is important for you to develop a working program by developing steps to replace the false assumptions. This can be as follows:
   - *Setting realistic goals and writing them down.*
   - *Visualizing your goals. This is especially when your conscious rational mind can be influenced easily.*
   - *Learn to affirm yourself. This builds self confidence and self esteem.*
   - *Replace lack-thinking with probability-thinking that is, increasing your chances of success by trying harder and acquiring the right skills.*
9. **Invest in people**:-Any business or organization is only as good as the personnel who manage it. When you invest in any venture, remember you are investing in the character of the people managing it.

10. Before investing, investigate:-Integrity is the essence of character, faithfulness is the cornerstone. Before investing look deep into your spirit and see whether there is peace. ***An internal witness is better than an external witness.***

11. Risk but don't gamble:-Learn and know the seasons. Gather as much information as possible about the investment before you can commit yourself.

12. It must be in writing:-Anything spelled on paper is reliable.***Onassis once commented" I feel so sad when people don't practice to write down anything because they will always forget".***

13. Stop living in a grave:-If you lose an investment, bury it. People who failed once and refuse to try again live with death. Learn to live, bury your past failures and not the talents you still have. Admit your loss, learn from it and go on to do better things. ***Don't carry your mistakes like a carcass.***

14. Invest in producers:-Invest your time with people who inspire. Invest your money with people who inspire. Invest your money with people who produce. Invest your gifts, talents and skills with people who create.

15. Shadows are more fierce than reality:-People who borrow and don't repay suffer from guilt. Guilty casts a big shadow. ***Guilt is a killer***. Learn to forgive ***yourself and others. Live a free life.***

16. Wealth comes from friends:-You should be more concerned with making friends more than customers. Business comes from those who feel friendly towards you. Any investment to make a friend will pay great dividends.

17. Don't quit:- ***"Never quit. Quitters never win and winners never quit".*** -Just keep plaguing along until it works for you. If others are saying it can't be done, you are going to feel such immense satisfaction at actually doing it that your confidence will soar.

18. Goal setting:-Goal setting is the first most important fundamental step in the wealth creation process. When you have a specific goal, the rest of the planning process falls into place. But before setting your goals***, find out what you are standing on. This is in: where you are, where you want to go and how you plan to get there.***

19. Understand risks involved:-All wealth creation decisions involve a balancing act between the return you need for your investments and the risk you are prepared to accept. ***Are you aware that savings accounts can actually generate negative returns over the long-term?***

20. Good debt verses bad debt: -While debt can at times be viewed in negative light, it can be an effective method to increase your net wealth if used for the right purposes in the right way. Borrowing money to purchase assets which will continue to produce an income can be considered "good debt" because it has the ability to increase your net wealth overtime and help you towards a financially secure future. "False wealth" consists of depreciating lifestyle asset such as cars, fancy clothes, and consumer items. These type of purchases will not produce an income they will depreciate (reduce) in value and will actually generate extra expenses.

Life is an adventure worth living. I encourage you to learn and to swim upstream.

Topic 4:

BARRIERS TO WEALTH CREATION:

"Wealth is when small efforts produce large results, whereas poverty is when large efforts produce small results."

1. **A lack of clear focus in what you really want to do**. Focusing on money as the main motivator in the business activities.
2. **Not setting up clear systems** of internal control in your business.
3. **Wrong assumptions about wealth**.
    - Having a good job and heads ultimately to wealth. The job supports our habits such as eating, rent & maintaining our standards of living, but merely leads to wealth creation.
    - Saving money is a good investment-It is important to wealth creation process-since it creates discipline which is a key component to wealth creation-But the interest rates offered by the banks are not enough-It is a slow liquidation of money because of inflation and taxes.
    - Debt is bad avoid it like a plague-Avoid consumer debt plague. This is borrowing money to buy the appearance of wealth. These are things which lose value and are often worthless before the debt is repaid.
    - Security is good-Job security is an illusion. It is dangerous to assume that security is good. The more you love security the more likely you avoid risk. If you avoid risk you also avoid opportunity because, risk is the price you pay for opportunity. You can't hate risk & hope for freedom. Learn to view risk positively as an essential step in the road to wealth creation.

- Failure is bad-Mature people realize that failure is part of success. If you develop a positive attitude about failure you can bear a great deal from it. It helps you to develop ingenuity (new ways & methods of doing things), flexibility and an ability to create new ways of achieving goals. Failure can teach you more about success than four years at the best university.

Do you know of a successful person who has risen to the top without some failure? Failure can be the best thing that ever happened to you. Wealth is not money alone. Money is just the appearance of wealth, the form but not the substance. ***Wealth is a thought, not things.*** You can be rich and not wealth.

Wealth is an attitude, a state of mind. Being broke is a temporary condition but ***being poor is a state of mind.***

- **Someone else is responsible for my financial well-being**:-Many people have ceased to assume personal responsibility for their financial well being and assume the government, employer, parents are responsible. The sooner you realize that you are responsible for your financial welfare the better for you. **WHY?** ***You are 100% responsible for your life because you cannot control the wind neither can you control the season but, you can change yourself and increase your wealth generation process. This is within your control.***
- **Acquiring wealth is a win/lose game.** This has been assumed as a dirty business in which the ***acquirer*** takes advantage of the ***acquiree*** in some illegal and immoral way. People think that you must be greedy in order to make money. In reality there is an infinite source of wealth. The key is learning how to tap it through

creating business deals that add value to each party in the transaction. None has to lose in order for you to be wealthy or create wealth.

- **It takes money to make money**-You can become wealth starting from where you are now. The principle of leverage and borrowing can help you create personal wealth. This principle means that we have so many assets that we can employ. They are financial and non-financial assets. Financial assets are like credit, cash from your net worth. Your net worth is the difference between assets minus your ability. Your financial assets will include good relationships, ideas, time and the courage to venture in an enterprise.
- **Lack of taking responsibility**:-Pointing fingers outside yourself for anything that happens to you is itself a lack of being responsible for your life. This means you don't ask yourself the key success creating questions which are:
    1. ***What did I do or not do in order for this situation to arise?***
    2. ***What did I say or not say for this situation to arise?***

    Answers to these questions propel you to discover your contribution on the issue at hand and take the necessary corrective measures. It also helps you improve your unique wealth generosity areas as you know what you need to do.
- **Ignorance and lack of learning**:-When we decide to become flexible, keep an open mind and learn, chances are that we will become wealthy.

Indeed a learned person solves problems and creates wealth.

There are stories of lottery winners who are poor and suddenly become rich and poor again.

The reason to it is that as much as they have stuck a jackpot, they have a poverty mindset that cannot generate income from what they already have, but spend with a consumptive approach, which always leads to lack.

- **Lack of character**:-If you lack character, it means that nobody can have confidence in you hence opportunities will be running away from you because, wealth comes through relationships. ***Don't forget that you are a priceless asset in the wealth creation process. Your character, which is constituted in the following elements: - honesty, integrity, truthfulness and accountability-*** Plays a key role in the wealth creation process.
- **Uncooperative spouse**:-Another barrier to wealth creation includes:-Having an uncooperative spouse. This is a very sensitive area and requires a lot of wisdom. The reason that a person without stable family cannot claim to be wealthy. Look and ask yourself the specific areas you feel your spouse is an obstacle to you brighter future.

Questions to ask:

- ***Does he or she spend too much money, refuse to talk about it, has limited money skills or has different financial goals?*** It is advisable to appreciate your spouse personality make up and background.

- Insufficient knowledge about money:-Money and money management can also be a barrier to wealth creation. Money has feelings and it will always treat you right if you respect it. A person who uses it rightly will always attract more money. One who misuses money in activities that don't add value will always find money running away from him. It's therefore important to know more about money management.
- **Doing "what you are not"-Being misplaced:-**Have you ever asked yourself whether you are in the right profession? Consider it wisdom to ask yourself continuously whether what you are doing is suited to your talents, skills, experience and desires. If what you are doing does not meet this criterion, allow yourself to start thinking whether you require additional training or start networking with friends for opportunities in the areas that you function well.
- **Fear:-**The self talk which occurs in our sub-conscious mind especially when we want to make a choice that will change our lives radically, are key barriers to wealth creation. Some of this are:
    1. ***If I will achieve that goal, I will stop being myself. I will lose personality.*** Appreciate that in life you must constantly change because that is what keeps us growing. Also know that with growth you become a wonderful person, both spiritually and materially.
    2. ***"I am not worth it.*** *I don't deserve to be successful"*-In respect to this, it is important to admit that you have low self - esteem. Be honest with yourself and look for ways of self-development in order to boost your self esteem.

3. ***"It is impossible"*** -In respect to this, start using the golden rule that says: "if someone else can do it, why not me". Learn to follow other people's examples while making the end product unique to you. ***You have to free the great thinker and the great fighter in you who says " I can do it"***
4. ***"The goal is not worth my effort"*** -There is a tendency/habit of assuming and looking down on some project either by pride or underrating yourself, which leads you not to take some activities that can lead you to a better future. Do not discard the project at this moment. Tackle the challenge of pride or esteem and then enjoy the activity. It is advisable to start concentrating on things that make you happy.

Topic 5:

PRINCIPLES OF SUCCESS: How to fashion your own brand of success:

There are two main criteria of success:

1. Do others think you are a success?
2. Do you think so yourself? These two are related as the straw is related to the ice ream soda. If you really want to fully enjoy an ice cream soda it is nice to have both. It is useless, worthless and futile too, to have the whole world thinking that you are a success if you do not think so yourself. ***"The big question is whether you are going to say a hearty yes to your adventure" Said Joseph Campbell.*** Also it is good to remember this "Whether ***you think you can or think you cant you are right"-said Henry Ford.***

The ice cream of success is **your inward knowledge of it.** Given that you do not necessarily need acknowledgement of the outside world. The trouble comes when we try to ***fashion our success to the outside world's specifications even though this are not the specifications drawn up in our hearts. (Inside us……. The real "we"…. the real "you").***

The question is: **For whom are we succeeding, for ourselves or for somebody else?**

Success, if it has to be meaningful, it has to be a personal thing. ***Your real world is a giant negotiating table, and like it or not, you are a participant***-**Said Herb Cohen in his book: You can negotiate anything.** Personal success ***must exist inside*** if it is to exist at all. It cannot be composed of outward signs or appearances, ***but only of the intangible personal values stemming from a mature philosophy.***

Take the example of the richest men who ever lived by material possessions and formidably wealth: Andrew Carnegie, Jacob Riis, Julius Rosenwald, Samwel Mather, and The Guggenheims & Russell Sage. All these men achieved true personal success.

In these cases, outward as well as inward.

Constant factors to be found in true success:

1. The first constant factor is **Purpose.** One must understand that in whatever he/she does he/she is moving towards a **Goal.**

   Aimlessness is the worst enemy of success. *Who you are makes a difference. Everybody can be great because anybody can serve. You don't have to have a college degree to serve, you don't have to make your subject and verbs agree to serve. You only need a heart full of grace. A soul generated by love said Dr.Martin Luther King Jnr.* One can hardly feel successful in a bog. As long as one has a purpose he/she feels that his/her **energies** and **creative thought** are taking him somewhere and there is **satisfaction** in the journey. Just as there is despair whenever we feel, as often as insightfully put it, that we are getting anywhere. "To **be a nobody is to be everybody".** Success to be true must have **an abiding sense of purpose,** or otherwise, though one may vegetate successfully, one cannot live successfully.
2. Success has the **intrinsic character of abetting average.** It is not all a piece; not every hour nor every day is uniformly successful. Rather there are upturns in success separated by valleys of failure.

3. **Successful life will have its days or even years of failure.** It will certainly have its moments of utter washout. This are not blights upon such a life but merely the inevitable failings which bear testimony to the fact that success isn't easy.

In growing up each one of us must learn sooner or later that every day isn't Christmas, and so in courting success we must learn too, that every effort cannot be crowned with glory. However, don't worry about failure, worry about chances you miss when you don't even try. ***The sense of obligation to continue is present in all of us. A duty to strive is the duty of us all. I felt a call to that duty-said Abraham Lincoln.***

You should as well understand that ***obstacles are those things you see when you take your eyes off your goal- said Henry Ford. It's better to be prepared for an opportunity and not have one, than to have an opportunity and not be prepared said Whitney Young Jnr.***

4. The third constant ingredient of success **is the price of it.** There is no success for free. One of the wondrous aspects of these lives of ours, a somewhat mystical aspect, is our constitutional inability to enjoy what we have not earned or labored for. The joy of success, it seems, must be counter balanced by the effort to achieve it- and that's a mystical little aspect of human character which exists in all of us. **"Out of great tension may come great harmony"** said Theodore E.Steinwey-President of Steinway & sons. We know that everything we need to know to end the needless emotional suffering that many people currently experience.

High self-esteem & personal effectiveness is available to anyone willing to take the time to pursue it. "**The only difference between an ordinary man and a warrior is that a warrior takes everything as a challenge, while an ordinary man takes everything either as a blessing or a curse-**said Don Juan.

Our lives are a continuing journey- and we must learn and grow at every bend as we make our way sometimes stumbling, but always moving towards the ***finest within us***- (***Power of optimism:-By Allan McGinnis).***

5. The fourth essential ingredient, without which success is not success, is **Satisfaction.** One man's meat is one's poison, and so satisfaction to one man, may stem from the amassing of fortune, while to another man, it may come from writing of a poem. But certainly neither man can claim success at all if there is no satisfaction in either the fortune or the poem. Success must be enjoyed. It may be won with tears, but it must be crowned with laughter.

Otherwise, the effort may be worthwhile-It may be good or even great but for the individual **without the inner laughter, which is known by another name as SATISFACTION,** there can hardly be success.

The serious anomaly of our times is that many people ***have all the outward trappings of success*** without the ***essential inner trappings of it.*** They don't feel success; ***instead of warmth inside, there is barrenness***. "I **have worked and slaved and acknowledged myself out- for what?** Has become the refrain.

The satisfaction of success need to be identifiable by any one else or to any one else so long as the person himself knows it is there. Satisfaction, stemming largely from an attitude, is available to all in that it begins **inside,** a kind of **central nugget deep in the strata of our souls.**

6. A final basic element of success is **Spirituality**. It is hard to imagine anyone feeling successful without also feeling related **somehow to the greater purposes of life and to the author of those purposes.** Whether one is a success hobo or a successful banker, he must, if he is to sense the full bouquet of success, have conviction, however subtle, that he is in **tune with God**. He must sense somehow the pervasive currents of God's existence and recognize his own existence and in those currents too.

   All you need to realize and understand well is that success is no straight jacket. It is no mold into which all must be poured. It is no rigid stamp. It is as individual as our fingertips or the look in our eyes. All we need is the courage to be and realize ourselves.

Topic 6:

Agile entrepreneurship:

10 Rules to Succeed In Business

"There will come a time when big opportunities will be presented to you and you've got to be in a position to take advantage of them".

Sam Walton, founder of Wal-Mart, grew up poor in a farm community in rural Missouri during the great depression. The poverty he experienced while growing up taught him the value of money and to persevere.

After attending the University of Missouri, he immediately worked for J.C Penny where he got first taste of retailing. He served in World War II after which he became a successful franchiser of Ben Franklin five-and dime stores. In 1962, he had the idea of opening bigger stores, sticking to rural areas, keeping costs low and discounting heavily.

The management disagreed with his vision. Undaunted, Walton pursued his vision, founded Wal-Mart and started a retailing success story. When Walton died in 1992 the family's net worth approached $ 25 billion.

Today, Wal-Mart is the world's number one retailer, with more than 4, 150 stores, including discount stores, combination discount and grocery stores, and membership-only ware house (Sam's Club).Learn Walton's winning formula for business".

If Sam Walton did it so you can.

Agile entrepreneurship is about launching businesses faster significantly reducing your odds of failure. It's about making your business successful, so you are free, to do what you want, when you want, where you want. Really, its about what you love and making money while you are doing it.

Lessons:

1. **Sam Walton followed his heart.**
2. **He was focused regardless of other external influences.**
3. **He loved what he was doing.**
4. **He never bothered on what people said.**
5. **He was the master and captain of his own ship.**
6. **He knew that he only had one life.**
7. **He knew he had a purpose.**
8. **He had re-examined himself:** The un examined life is not worth living.
9. **He had the courage, self esteem, motivation and the desire to continue existing with his vision.**

10. **He was responsible and determined to get the best of life before him.**

10 Rules of Agile Entrepreneurship:

Rule 1: Get the right people on the bus:

Putting your team together is one of the single most important things you need to do as an entrepreneur. You need a team of truly outstanding people. You need **A** players. And you are going to want to emphasize learning and experience to get them on board. Great people need to be challenged. They want to learn and grow. Strange as this may sound, money is rarely the top priority for them. If you offer a better and more dynamic work experience, you can get great people without having to pay ridiculous salaries. In addition, if you are looking for another founder, try to find someone who will compliment you weaknesses. You don't need another **YOU**. What you need is someone who excels at things you are not so good at or don't enjoy.

Rule 2: Know what mountain to climb:

This rule has to be one of the most valuable lessons one has to learn (and perhaps the most painful).If you and your team don't know where you are going then it will be impossible to reach your end goal. How can you possibly achieve your goal in the shortest amount of time, with least resources, if you are not clear about what you want to achieve? If you want smart people to follow you, they need to know where you are going. **"If you don't know where you are going any road will take you there)".**

Rule 3: Always think like a marketer:

You can put greatest product into the market with a belief that people would magically flock to it, and, of course, they'd go tell all their friends about it too. Many entrepreneurs look down at sales and marketing to their detriment. Don't make the same mistake. Sales and marketing orientation is the life blood of all successful business the world over. The bottom line is that if you want to be successful entrepreneur, you must pay attention to sales and marketing. Remember, if you believe in your product, there is nothing wrong with getting it to as many people as possible.

Rule 4: Ideas do NOT Matter; It is Execution that counts:

Honestly, any one can have a good idea. Its execution that counts, and this is the hard part getting organized, putting the pieces together, hammering out the details. This is what matters. At the same time, don't get planning paralysis. Learn more towards the Ready Fire, Aim approach. Execute quickly, early and often. And remember to celebrate every milestone of successes and failures. ***It's surprising that most people concentrate on celebrating success. When it comes to failure, they succumb to their graves of inability. The two complement each other and makes a meaning of existence in any business. Failures are the stepping stones to success. Your weaknesses and failures is a lesson.***

Rule 5: Set BIG Goals:

You need big goals. If a goal doesn't excite you and make you a little nervous, you need to think bigger. ***Stop trudging on the mad. You need to change your route map and try something else that is workable.***

Moreover, your team isn't going to be inspired or motivated by wimpy goals. Too many people toil away on the planning part and never really have the end goal in mind. Goal first, strategy later. You need to visualize your goals every day. Use a vision board to help you do this.

Rule 6: Know when to push and when to let go:

Getting from point **A** to point **B** is never a straight line. Sometimes, along the way, you will figure out that it's not even point **B** you are after. Its point **C**.Time to stop climbing one mountain and headed up another. Other times you know exactly where it is that you want to go, but your approach isn't working. Its time for a new line of attack. The point is to take a step back and get perspective every once and a while. If you can clearly see that what you are doing will get you up the right mountain, by all means push. Just be open to letting go, if you have to. Not everything you do is going to work. Yes, this sucks. Its no fun. Clean yourself off and get back in the game. And please learn from your mistakes. There's nothing worse than watching people make the same mistakes over and over. **"To keep doing the same thing while expecting different results is the definition of insanity"**

Rule 7: Learn to love systems, processes and numbers:

Systems, processes and numbers are the core of a well run company, especially one that can run on autopilot. Also remember to measure everything. When the business is your baby, your heart can be in too much. Numbers won't lie. Last thing: Make sure everyone in the company knows the numbers; nothing is more empowering than showing them the impact of their efforts.

Rule 8: Work on your business not in your business:

What exactly does this mean? It means you should constantly be delegating. If you are still buying the cookies for the office when you have a staff of more than 20 people, you must stop. Everything that is required to **RUN** your business should be delegated. ***What you should be doing is coming up with new ideas, innovations, products and markets. This is a role that should not be ignored. On the basis of this you will be able to map out good realizable strategies.***

You should be taking in the big picture and dividing in and out when your direct attention is required. Stop micro-managing and trust people. If you really don't trust your team, you need to get new people on your bus.

Rule 9: Always be learning and experimenting:

If you are not growing, you are dying. The most successful people do three simple things:

1) **They always learn new things.**
2) **They always try new things.**
3) **They never give up.** Hunger for knowledge is everything; it can completely change the company. Encourage your staff to spend 10% of their time on learning and developing their work-related skills. Doing this will change your company. The person you had a meeting with last month will be a different person than the one you meet this month. It's not good to work in a boring place, so this emphasis on learning and experimentation keeps things hopping. (Never ***quit, quitters never WIN & winners never quit).***

Rule 10: Do what you love and love what you do:

Follow your heart.(***Most of us live in vacuums of doubt and suspicion, mistrust and disbelief. Following your heart is the key to success).*** Cheesy, but true, if it's your calling to start a mountain climbing school on the slopes of mount Kenya, go for it. If you love it, you will probably make good living doing it, and you can visit home any time you want. ***You only have one life.*** What point is there in living it for someone else? When you are doing what you're supposed to be doing, it doesn't really feel like work. From my experience, it feels more like a game.

There are so many people out there trapped in this idea of what life should be: 8 - to - 5 for forty something years and then a few years of retirement. Life is about experiences and giving back. Take stock of your natural strengths and what you enjoy doing, this will help you carve out a life of joy, abundance and success.

Topic 7:

Case Study I:

A Beautiful Mind Attracts Wealth:

"Whatever you hold in your mind will tend to occur in your life. If you continue to believe as you have always believed, you will continue to act as you have always acted. If you continue to act as you have always acted, you will continue to get what you have always gotten. If you want different results in your life or your work, all you have to do is change your mind".

"There is this beautiful woman in the party. She has flawless skin, elegant clothes and a perfect figure. Surprisingly, she seems to be on her own. People, who come to her, quickly drift away.

Then there is a short, balding and mousy man. He is always surrounded by people in animated conversation with him.

What is going on?

You can do a great deal to make your body more beautiful. There are exercises at the gym. There are nips and tucks and liposuction and inserts.

You can do much to make your face more beautiful with cosmetics and even plastic surgery. A man can have hair implants, but what about your mind? Do you make any effort at all to have a beautiful mind? Great physical beauty with a boring mind is boring. You might get attention but you will never keep that attention.

In this party, the beautiful woman had a boring mind and the mousy man had a beautiful mind. That is why the man got more attention than the woman.

One of the things you can do in order to attract wealth in your life is to develop a beautiful mind. As you grow older physical beauty tends to fade. But beauty of the mind is independent of age and can actually increase with wisdom and experience. Spend time and effort to make your mind more beautiful. Having a beautiful mind is not solving complex situations and puzzles. It is simply having a mind that can be appreciated by others, usually through conversation. The beauty of your mind shows in your conversation. And what a great resource of creating your wealth!

A beautiful mind is created through:

1. **Learning how to agree:-**This is done by genuinely seeking points of agreements in all conversations. That is by **creating a win-win** situation for everyone. As well as **seeking to understand in order to be understood**. It is by appreciating that you don't need to be right all the time. Always remove your ego from all discussions and focus on the subject matter. This means that you have got to always see the other persons view point and where he is coming from.
2. **Learn to be interesting: -** Through the way you conduct a conversation. It is injecting new ideas into a discussion through making connections.

3. **<u>The ability to listen and the enjoyment of listening:</u>-This is a key element in** developing a beautiful mind. Seek to get maximum value from what is being said. Emotions and feelings are very important part of our thinking. Our choices and decisions are based on them. In discussions, it is important to listen first, ask questions before showing your feelings. Realize that you do not need full and complete information about the subject. At times all that is required is to listen intelligently and ask questions.

Case study II:

Learning -The shortest distance between wealth and Poverty.

" You can teach a student a lesson for a day; but you can teach him to learn by creating curiosity, he will continue the learning process as long as he lives"-Clay P. Bedford.

Taking in information (education) is a distance relative of real learning. If i read a great book about bicycle riding, can i ride a bicycle?

Learning involves a fundamental shift or movement of mind. Learning involves getting into the heart of what it means to human. Through learning we re-create ourselves, we are able to do something we never were able to do and we re-perceive the world and our relationship to it.

Through learning, we extend our capacity to create. The truth is that, within each one of us, there is a deep hunger for this type of learning. This type of learning is as fundamental to human beings as the sex drive.

The basic meaning of learning is to continually expand our capacity to create the future; a wealthy future.

In contrast to insects, it is said that human beings start out as butterflies and end up in cocoons. Look around you and see how middle aged people are pessimistic about life and diminished every day in great numbers, too great to bear thinking about. They are forced through an educational system that stunts their capacity for a life time of growth. The education system should teach them how to devise solutions to changing problems.

The education experience should teach us long term wealth-creation methods, teach us to be creative and also teach us how to devise solutions to problems.

I must admit that proper credentials are important but the ability to create solutions for your life is critically important.

My reader Iam trying to talk to you and tell you that for you to create wealth in your life you must learn the following:

How the economy works, finance and business management, the free market system, about the right to fail, need for sacrifice, individual responsibility and importance of following one's dream and turning it into reality.

The seminar format is a modern vehicle for adult learning. **Why?** This is because the adult coming to a seminar is generally thirst to learn more, and is more concerned with obtaining specific answers to specific problems. At a seminar, a participant can engage in a two way transfer of information not only with instructor, but also with fellow participants. They can hear testimonies, ask questions and diffuse insecurities. They can also establish channels of friendship and people to call incase of an emergency.

It is important to learn from experts but don't be copy cat because hero worship is one sign of poverty mindedness.

Remain the unique you. This means you become your own expert after collecting the wisdom of other experts. ***But remember, you are still responsible for incorporating your wealth creating investment framework. It is your duty to create your own route to success.***

After you have been taught, become the best teacher of yourself. **Motivate yourself, break camp and move up the mountains.** ***The best teacher is not a camp maker but a camp breaker.***

Learning means everything for you to succeed.

Chapter 4:

A more imaginative you:

"Imagination grows by exercise, and, contrary to common belief, is more powerful in the mature than the young" said Somerset Maugham.

Avoid the error or mentality of thinking that a good imagination is the possession solely of children and people like writers and artists. In fact imagination is part of everyone's mental equipment and can be developed to advantage. ***Dreamers are the partakers of the world!***

www.ingramcontent.com/pod-product-compliance
Ingram Content Group UK Ltd.
Pitfield, Milton Keynes, MK11 3LW, UK
UKHW041926190726
13854UKWH00003B/1469